greatest
artists

Michelangelo

Jennifer Howse

MEDIA ENHANCED BOOKS
AV2 BY WEIGL™
ADDED VALUE • AUDIO VISUAL

www.av2books.com

AV² provides enriched content that supplements and complements this book. Weigl's AV² books strive to create inspired learning and engage young minds in a total learning experience.

Your AV² Media Enhanced books come alive with...

Audio
Listen to sections of the book read aloud.

Key Words
Study vocabulary, and complete a matching word activity.

Video
Watch informative video clips.

Quizzes
Test your knowledge.

Go to **www.av2books.com**, and enter this book's unique code.

Embedded Weblinks
Gain additional information for research.

Slide Show
View images and captions, and prepare a presentation.

BOOK CODE

Y824389

AV² **by Weigl** brings you media enhanced books that support active learning.

Try This!
Complete activities and hands-on experiments.

... and much, much more!

Published by AV² by Weigl
350 5th Avenue, 59th Floor
New York, NY 10118
Website: www.av2books.com

Library of Congress Cataloging-in-Publication Data

Names: Howse, Jennifer, author.
Title: Michelangelo / Jennifer Howse.
Description: New York : AV2 by Weigl, 2016. | Series: Greatest artists |
   Includes index.
Identifiers: LCCN 2016004395 (print) | LCCN 2016005071 (ebook) | ISBN
   9781489646231 (hard cover : alk. paper) | ISBN 9781489650337 (soft cover :
   alk. paper) | ISBN 9781489646248 (Multi-user ebk.)
Subjects: LCSH: Michelangelo Buonarroti, 1475-1564—Juvenile literature. |
   Artists—Italy—Biography—Juvenile literature.
Classification: LCC N6923.B9 H76 2016 (print) | LCC N6923.B9 (ebook) | DDC
   709.2—dc23
LC record available at http://lccn.loc.gov/2016004395

Printed in the United States of America in Brainerd, Minnesota
1 2 3 4 5 6 7 8 9 0 20 19 18 17 16

032016
210316

Editor: Heather Kissock   Art Director: Terry Paulhus

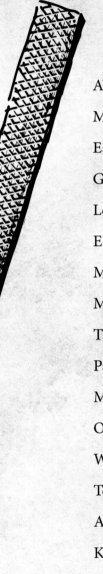

CONTENTS

Meet Michelangelo

Even though Michelangelo is considered one of the greatest artists of all time, he was a perfectionist who was very critical of his own work.

Michelangelo Buonarroti was a creator of art and architecture whose fierce ambition inspired him to create some of the world's greatest masterpieces. Even today, people travel to Europe just to see the evidence of his artistry. The city of Florence, Italy, is graced with many of Michelangelo's creations, as are Rome and Vatican City.

Considered one of the greatest artists of the **Renaissance**, Michelangelo drew, painted, and sculpted his works of art more than 500 years ago. He lived during a time of cultural rebirth in Europe, when there was a renewed interest in education, science, and the arts. The Renaissance is known as a period of intense artistic expression and scientific discovery. Italy, in particular, flourished during this period.

Lorenzo de' Medici was the ruler of Florence in the late 1400s and a fervent supporter of the Renaissance movement. With his support, arts and culture flourished in the city.

The Renaissance was an exciting time to be an artist, as opportunities to create were numerous, especially for those with talent. Such was the case for Michelangelo. His paintings and sculptures celebrate the human form and experience. His architectural designs pay tribute to the period of artistic rebirth in which he lived. Italy, and the world of art, would not be what they are today without his artistic contributions.

Florence is often referred to as the birthplace of the Renaissance. It is here that many of the early advances in art and science took place.

Early Life

M ichelangelo di Lodovico Buonarroti Simoni was born on March 6, 1475, in the town of Caprese, Italy. He was the second of five sons born to Leonardo di Buonarroti Simoni, a magistrate, and his wife, Francesca di Neri del Miniato di Siena. Buonarroti Simoni was once a noble name in Italy and a source of pride for Michelangelo's family. Unfortunately, by the time Michelangelo was born, the family had lost much of its social standing.

Shortly after Michelangelo was born, the family moved to the city of Florence. Michelangelo, however, was sent to live with his nurse and her family in the town of Settignano. The nurse's husband was a stonemason by trade. Michelangelo would later say that growing up in this environment inspired his interest in working with stone.

Today, the house in which Michelangelo was born serves as a museum. Visitors can see the artist's birth certificate and several reproductions of his art.

Michelangelo's mother died when he was six years old. Shortly after her death, his father remarried. Leonardo wanted his family to be reunited and requested that Michelangelo return to Florence. The family lived together in a house near the Santa Croce quarter, on the east side of the city.

Michelangelo attended a nearby grammar school, but he showed little interest in learning about reading or writing. Instead, he preferred to draw, and would spend his spare time watching local artisans build and paint churches and other buildings. His father did not approve of Michelangelo's interest in art. He encouraged his son to focus on his schooling.

> **"The science of design, or of line-drawing, if you like to use this term, is the source and very essence of painting, sculpture, architecture."**

Growing Up

While at school, Michelangelo became friends with a young painter named Francesco Granacci. Six years older than Michelangelo, Granacci was working in a paint shop owned by brothers Domenico and David Ghirlandaio. Granacci introduced Michelangelo to the brothers and told them about his young friend's interest in art. The brothers invited the 13-year-old Michelangelo to become an **apprentice** in their workshop. By this time, Michelangelo's father realized that his son was not going to embark on a traditional career. He gave Michelangelo permission to begin working with the Ghirlandaio brothers. Both artists were portrait painters, so Michelangelo learned the art of portrait painting as part of his training. He also helped them in the painting of **frescoes**.

The Ghirlandaio brothers painted portraits of many of Florence's leading citizens, including Giovanna Tornabuoni, a local noblewoman.

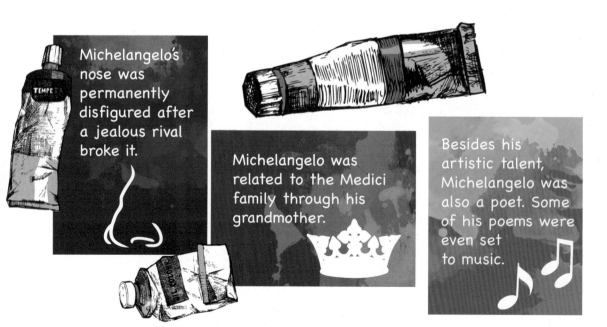

Michelangelo's nose was permanently disfigured after a jealous rival broke it.

Michelangelo was related to the Medici family through his grandmother.

Besides his artistic talent, Michelangelo was also a poet. Some of his poems were even set to music.

Domenico Ghirlandaio realized that Michelangelo was a talented artist. He recommended Michelangelo to Lorenzo de' Medici, the ruler of Florence, and asked that the young artist be given the opportunity to study the sculptures at the Medici palace. Lorenzo agreed, and Michelangelo moved into the palace to continue his apprenticeship. Living in the palace gave Michelangelo an opportunity to meet the great scholars and artists of Florence. They taught him about **philosophy** and the workings of government.

> "A man paints with his brains and not with his hands."

Michelangelo also became acquainted with the Augustinian friars of the Church of the Holy Spirit. This group of holy men supported the arts and young artists. The friars helped Michelangelo by providing **cadavers** for him to study. The human body fascinated Michelangelo. He applied his newly acquired knowledge of anatomy to the creation of his art.

The Boboli Gardens are located behind the Pitti Palace, the seat of the Medici family. The gardens hold a collection of statues that are based on Roman myths.

Bertoldo di Giovanni was best known for his bronze sculptures. However, he also worked with other materials, including terracotta, or glazed earthenware.

Learning the Craft

During his time at the palace, Michelangelo came into contact with Bertoldo di Giovanni, the keeper of the Medici collection of ancient sculptures. A sculptor himself, Giovanni taught Michelangelo the art of creating form and expression from blocks of stone. Some of Michelangelo's early sculptures, such as *Madonna of the Stairs* and *Battle of the Centaurs*, survive to this day.

Michelangelo enjoyed his time at the palace. He thrived as a student of art and appreciated the guidance of his various **mentors**. However, in 1492, Lorenzo de' Medici died, bringing an end to Michelangelo's apprenticeship. He left the palace and began to build a new life for himself.

Michelangelo created works of art for nine different Roman Catholic popes.

Over time, people began to call Michelangelo *Il Divino*, or "The Divine One," for his artistic contributions.

At least two of Michelangelo's works feature the artist's likeness. He placed himself in *Last Judgment* and in *The Deposition*.

One of the statues sculpted for the Basilica of San Domenico was of St. Proculus, a former soldier who became the protector of Bologna.

Michelangelo's travels took him to Venice and then to Bologna, where he continued to seek opportunities to study literature and sculpture. It was during this time that Michelangelo also started to receive **commissions** for his work. In Bologna, he was asked to sculpt three statues for the Basilica of San Domenico. He also sculpted a marble statue of Hercules for a family in Florence. By 1495, Michelangelo had returned to Florence, where he created a statue of St. John. Within the year, however, he decided to move to Rome.

As one of the largest cities in Italy, Rome was an ideal place for Michelangelo to launch his career as a professional artist. One of his sculptures, however, brought his reputation into question. Michelangelo had sculpted a statue of the Greek god Eros. Someone decided to damage the statue to make it look older than it was. The statue was bought by a church official, who later realized that it was not the ancient work of art it was said to be. The official demanded his money back, but also acknowledged Michelangelo's skill as an artist. He commissioned Michelangelo to create two other works, becoming the artist's first **patron** in Rome.

When Michelangelo moved to Rome, the city was experiencing a period of rebuilding, organized by a succession of popes. Many of the greatest artists of the Renaissance were commissioned to help with the design and construction of new buildings.

Early Achievements

A sculpture completed in 1499 sparked the beginning of Michelangelo's professional career. Entitled *Pietà* and carved from one block of marble, it is a religious work showing Mary holding Jesus Christ on her lap. The sculpture was commissioned by Cardinal Jean de Bilhères. It was to be placed in a small chapel in Vatican City's St. Peter's Basilica. Michelangelo was paid 450 ducats, or about $70,000, for the finished work. This payment made him one of the best-paid artists of his time, even though he was only in his mid-twenties.

The sculpture was an immediate success and brought Michelangelo much recognition. He remained in Rome for another two years. In 1501, however, Michelangelo decided to return to Florence. He had been asked to complete a work that had been started by another artist. The sculpture was to be of a hero from the Bible named David. Like *Pietà*, it was to be carved out of a single block of marble.

The statue of David was sculpted from Carrara marble, considered one of the whitest marbles in the world.

The work was intense, and the hours were long. By 1504, however, Michelangelo had completed the larger-than-life, 17-foot-tall (5.2 meters) sculpture. In recognition of the magnificence of the sculpture, *David* was placed in the center of Florence, at the Piazza della Signoria in front of the Palazzo Vecchio.

The statue of David solidified Michelangelo's reputation as a great artist. His skills as a sculptor were in high demand, and he created several more sculptures. As busy as he was, Michelangelo also continued to draw and paint. He still felt he had much to learn about art. Michelangelo studied and worked hard to perfect his techniques. He liked to work alone and was very secretive about his plans for future projects. He would often send his drawings and plans to his family for safekeeping.

Even though Michelangelo's studio was only a short distance away, it took 40 men four days to move *David* into the Piazza della Signoria.

Master Class

Michelangelo often described himself as a self-taught artist. Although he was influenced by other artists early in his career, he had his own ideas about art and his own unique ways of approaching a project. This allowed him to turn the techniques he learned from others into his own.

Satyr's Head

Cross-Hatching

Cross-hatching is a drawing technique used to show light and shadow. It involves drawing a series of parallel lines across the paper and then drawing another set of lines over them, usually in a perpendicular direction. The number of lines and their distance from each other creates depth and adds to the shape of the figure being drawn. This technique was used by Michelangelo to create volume and solidity in his sketches of the human body.

Fresco Painting

Fresco painting is a tradition in Italy. Most artists, including Michelangelo, received training in this art form. Fresco painting uses **plaster**. Three coats of this plaster, along with sand and marble, are applied to the painting surface. A **stencil** is then used to map out the picture to be painted. The paint is applied before the plaster dries. The particles in the paint bind to the plaster, setting the paint so that it remains permanently in the plaster. Michelangelo used this technique throughout his career. His best-known frescoes are found on the ceiling of the Vatican's Sistine Chapel.

Erithraea

The Deposition

Modeling

Models played an important role in Michelangelo's sculpting process. After sketching a plan for a statue, he would sculpt a miniature version of it out of terracotta and show it to his client. Once this version was approved, Michelangelo sculpted a small version of the statue out of wax. He would then lay the wax sculpture in a tank of water, gradually releasing water from the tank to expose pieces of the sculpture. Michelangelo would carve what he saw on the wax figure into the marble block that was to become the final statue.

Cangiantismo

The technique of using contrasting colors in painting is called cangiantismo. During the Renaissance, painters perfected cangiantismo in both **tempera** and fresco paintings. They would use bright and contrasting colors to create highlights and lowlights in the folds of drapery. Michelangelo was a master of this technique. He created dramatic shifts between light and dark by using colors such as turquoise-violet and orange-blue. This technique can be seen in the painting of the prophet Ezekiel on the ceiling of the Sistine Chapel. The shoulder and knee of the prophet are lightened with white to create an effect of movement and three-dimensional form.

Ezekiel

Major Works

Michelangelo's artistry was not limited to one type of art. He was multi-talented and able to create art in a variety of forms. The art world is all the richer for his contributions to sculpture, painting, and architecture.

Madonna of the Stairs

Madonna of the Stairs is believed to be one of the first sculptures Michelangelo ever carved. The sculpture shows the Madonna sitting on a stone block with her robes wrapped around her. She holds her baby in her arms. The baby is also wrapped in the cloak, facing toward his mother and away from the viewer. In the background, four young men hold a long piece of cloth, believed to be a shroud. Even though Michelangelo was only about 17 years old when he created *Madonna of the Stairs*, the sculpture demonstrates his skill at shallow **relief** carving. Some art historians have said that the details added to the sculpture look more like the work of a pencil than a chisel.

DATE: 1490 to 1492 **MEDIUM:** Marble **SIZE:** 22.3 × 15.8 inches (56.7 × 40.1 centimeters)

Pietá

Michelangelo's *Pietá* shows Mary holding her son, Jesus Christ, following his crucifixion. The artist has draped the Mary figure in delicate folds of fabric. The sinewy realism of well-defined muscle in the Christ figure provides a sensitive beauty to the piece.

The sculpture was unique for the time because Renaissance sculptors usually focused their attention on only one subject. However, in sculpting Mary and her son, Michelangelo positioned the two figures so they create a unified whole. The sculpture itself forms a pyramid, a shape found in many artworks from the Renaissance.

DATE: 1499 **MEDIUM:** Marble **SIZE:** 68.5 × 76.8 inches (174 × 195 cm)

Doni Tondo

Sometimes called the Holy Family, *Doni Tondo* is a circular tempera painting showing Joseph, Mary, and the baby Jesus on a patch of grass. Mary sits in the **foreground** of the painting, while Joseph stands behind her. Both parents are shown caring for their young child.

Doni Tondo is often referenced as the beginning of a style called Mannerism. Common in later Renaissance works, Mannerist paintings are known for their bright colors and the unnatural poses of their subjects. In the painting, Mary turns backward to reach for the baby, creating a spiral movement within the work. The painting is displayed in a wooden frame that Michelangelo is believed to have helped design.

DATE: 1506 to 1508 **MEDIUM:** Oil and tempera on panel **SIZE:** 47.24 inches (120 cm) in diameter

Basilica of St. Mary of the Angels and Martyrs

Michelangelo was commissioned to design the Basilica of St. Mary of the Angels and Martyrs by Pope Pius IV. The artist died before the church could be completed, but his architectural plans were still used in its construction. The basilica was Michelangelo's last major architectural work.

Built over ancient Roman baths, the basilica is based upon a Greek cross floor plan. This means that its four arms are all the same length. The outside of the basilica is considered quite plain for Renaissance architecture. The true beauty of the building is only discovered upon entering through the huge bronze doors. Red granite columns and **vaulted** ceilings provide the basilica with a richness and sense of grandeur.

DATE: 1561 **MEDIUM:** Mixed **SIZE:** 420 × 344 feet (128 x 105 m)

Timeline of Michelangelo

1475

Michelangelo is born on March 6 in Caprese, a small town outside of Florence, Italy. His father, Leonardo di Buonarroti Simoni, is a local magistrate.

1488

At the age of 13, Michelangelo is apprenticed to painters David and Domenico Ghirlandaio. Domenico later makes arrangements for Michelangelo to apprentice at the palace of Lorenzo de' Medici, in Florence.

1492

Lorenzo de' Medici dies, leaving Michelangelo without a patron. He decides to leave Florence in search of a new job.

1498

Cardinal Jean de Bilhères commissions Michelangelo to create a sculpture for St. Peter's Basilica, in Vatican City. Completed in 1499, the sculpture is named *Pietá*.

1501

Michelangelo receives a new commission to finish a sculpture started by another artist. The statue of David is completed in 1504 and displayed in central Florence.

1512

Michelangelo completes the painting of the Sistine Chapel's ceiling.

1534

After spending time in Florence, Michelangelo returns to Rome. Pope Clement VII commissions him to paint a new fresco for the Sistine Chapel. The work, called *Last Judgment*, is completed in 1541.

1564

Michelangelo dies in Rome at age 88, following a brief illness.

Path to Success

*I*n 1505, Michelangelo received a major commission from Pope Julius II. The pope wanted the artist to design and build his tomb. Michelangelo quickly began drawing plans for the massive project. He proposed a tomb that reached three stories high and was surrounded by 40 life-sized marble statues. However, before Michelangelo could begin sculpting the monument, the project was put on hold. The pope had decided he wanted Michelangelo to work on another project instead. Michelangelo was asked to paint the ceiling of the Sistine Chapel.

Michelangelo's frescoes cover 10,000 square feet (930 square meters) of the Sistine Chapel's ceiling.

At the time, the ceiling was painted blue and decorated with gold stars. Michelangelo worked closely with papal officials to plan a more complex and detailed work. Together, they decided that Michelangelo would paint frescoes of scenes from the Old Testament onto the ceiling panels.

Creating a work of this scope was a bold and ambitious challenge for Michelangelo. However, there were practical issues to overcome. Since the ceiling rises 68 feet (20.7 m) above the floor, Michelangelo had to find a way to access the ceiling to paint it. To do this, he created a scaffold that was held in place with brackets connected to the chapel's walls.

With his plans in place, Michelangelo began working on his masterpiece. However, his first attempt at painting the ceiling ended in frustration. Mold was discovered to be growing in the fresco plaster, and Michelangelo was forced to start again. Although the painstaking work was physically very hard on Michelangelo, he met all of the challenges and solved problems as they occurred. When the finished work was unveiled in October 1512, it was instantly recognized as one of the greatest works of art ever created.

The Creative Process

Artists are creative people. They have vivid imaginations and are able to think in abstract ways. Still, in order to create, they must have a process, or series of steps to follow. While most artists will adapt the process to suit their individual needs, there are basic steps that all artists use to plan and create their works.

Gathering Ideas
Observing and taking inspiration from surroundings

Researching
Studying the subject or topic to determine the approach

Forming Intent
Deciding on a subject or topic to explore

Planning the Work
Obtaining the materials needed to create the work

Outlining the Project
Sketching or developing a model to follow

Creating the Work
Applying the previous stages to the creation of the final product

Making Revisions
Changing elements that are not working

Requesting Feedback
Asking for opinions from others

Completing the Work

Michelangelo's Legacy

Michelangelo was only 37 years old when he completed the painting of the Sistine Chapel's ceiling. The success of this project ensured that he was never out of work. Michelangelo went on to design a variety of buildings, ranging from churches to a library, and even completed the tomb of Pope Julius II. He also continued to sculpt and paint, including a return to the Sistine Chapel to paint *Last Judgment* over the high altar in 1534. In 1546, he was named the chief architect of St. Peter's Basilica, a position he held until his death in 1564.

The 500th anniversary of Michelangelo's birth was celebrated in 1975. Many countries commemorated the celebration by issuing stamps and coins in the artist's honor.

The details of the life and works of Michelangelo are known today through his own words. Besides his poetry, Michelangelo also left a memoir of his life. Compiled by the writer Ascanio Condivi, the book is entitled *The Life of Michelangelo Buonarroti* and was published in 1553. Michelangelo also wrote letters to his family, which expressed his feelings and the challenges he faced in creating his art. These letters give details of his private life and friendships as well.

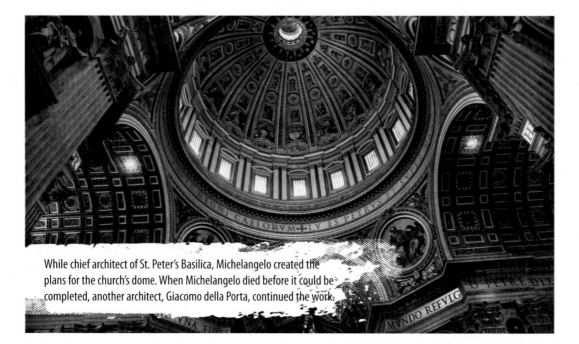

While chief architect of St. Peter's Basilica, Michelangelo created the plans for the church's dome. When Michelangelo died before it could be completed, another architect, Giacomo della Porta, continued the work.

However, Michelangelo's greatest legacy is his art. Not only did he leave behind masterpieces in architecture, sculpture, and painting, he also contributed to new forms of artistic expression. He was one of the first artists to create works in the Mannerist style. Many artists that came after Michelangelo continued this use of bold colors and unique poses.

Today, people continue to marvel at Michelangelo's creations. They visit the Sistine Chapel to see the ceiling and wander into Florence's Galleria dell'Accademia to experience the statue of David. Art students closely examine these works and others to absorb Michelangelo's techniques, with the hope of replicating them in their own creations.

Michelangelo was such a respected artist that other Renaissance painters sometimes included him in their own works. Such is the case in Raphael's *School of Athens*, which features Michelangelo as Heraclitus, a Greek philosopher.

Today, art students can hone their sculpting skills by recreating some of Michelangelo's best-known works.

On Display

Michelangelo's drawings, paintings, sculptures, and written works can be found in museums around the world. The pieces are highly valued parts of each museum's collection. Other works can still be viewed in the places for which they were created, in the context they were meant to serve.

The Louvre

The Louvre in Paris is one of the world's largest and greatest art galleries. Covering more than 650,000 square feet (60,387 sq. m), the museum's collection contains works from ancient times through to the 1800s. The Michelangelo gallery is located on the Louvre's ground floor. The gallery is devoted to Italian sculpture and features two of Michelangelo's works, *The Rebellious Slave* and *The Dying Slave*. Michelanglo began sculpting them for Pope Julius II's tomb, but never completed them. Today, they are prized pieces in the Louvre's sculpture collection.

The Louvre was initially a royal palace. It opened as a public art gallery on August 10, 1793.

Michelangelo's *David* is the star of the Galleria dell'Accademia's collection. There is often a long line of people waiting for their turn to enter the building.

Galleria dell'Accademia

Florence's Galleria dell'Accademia was founded in the 18th century. The first artworks to hang in the Galleria were from the Classical period. As time went on, works by more current artists were acquired. *David* became part of the Galleria's collection in 1873, when it was moved into the building from the Piazza della Signoria, where it had stood for almost 400 years. Today, the Galleria's collection also includes Michelangelo's *St. Matthew* and *Prisoners* statues.

Sistine Chapel

More than 5 million people visit the Sistine Chapel every year. Most come to view Michelangelo's interpretation of the Old Testament on the ceiling. However, the chapel also plays an important role in the Roman Catholic Church. It is where the papal conclave is held to vote for a new pope. The chapel is named after Pope Sixtus IV, who commissioned its construction to begin in 1475. From the outside, the building is plain in appearance. It is the interior that allows the building to shine. Along with the ceiling frescoes are wall murals and papal portraits painted by a series of well-known Italian artists.

Cardinals form a procession to enter the Sistine Chapel before a papal conclave. Once inside the chapel, they remain there until a new pope is elected.

Write a Biography

All of the parts of a biography work together to tell the story of a person's life. Find out how these elements come together by writing a biography. Begin by choosing a person whose story fascinates you. You will have to research the person's life by using library books and reliable websites. You can also email the person or write him or her a letter. The person might agree to answer your questions directly.

Use the chart below to guide you in writing the biography. Answer each of the questions listed using the information you have gathered. Each heading in the chart will form an important part of the person's story.

Parts of a Biography

Early Life
Where and when was the person born?
What is known about the person's family and friends?
Did the person grow up in unusual circumstances?

Growing Up
Who had the most influence on the person?
Did he or she receive assistance from others?
Did the person have a positive attitude?

Developing Skills
What was the person's education?
What was the person's first job or work experience?
What obstacles did the person overcome?

Early Achievements
What was the person's most important early success?
What processes does this person use in his or her work?
Which of the person's traits were most helpful in his or her work?

Leaving a Legacy
Has the person received awards or recognition for accomplishments?
What is the person's life's work?
How have the person's accomplishments served others?

Test Yourself

1

During which period of cultural rebirth did Michelangelo live?

Michelangelo lived during the Renaissance.

2

Where was Michelangelo born?

Michelangelo was born in Caprese, Italy.

3

Who were the portrait painters that Michelangelo apprenticed with?

Michelangelo apprenticed with Domenico and David Ghirlandaio.

4

Which member of the Florentine royal family allowed Michelangelo to study at his palace?

Lorenzo de' Medici let Michelangelo live and study in his palace.

5

Which keeper of the Medici sculpture collection did Michelangelo study under?

Michelangelo studied under Bertoldo di Giovanni, the keeper of the Medici sculpture collection.

6

What is the name of the 17-foot-tall (5.2-m) statue that Michelangelo sculpted?

David is the name of the 17-foot-tall (5.2-m) statue that Michelangelo sculpted.

7

Why do artists use the cross-hatching technique in their drawings?

Artists use the cross-hatching technique to show light and shadow.

8

What is another name for *Doni Tondo*?

Doni Tondo is also known as Holy Family.

9

What work was halted so Michelangelo could paint the Sistine Chapel's ceiling?

Michelangelo was asked to stop working on the tomb of Pope Julius II.

10

How old was Michelangelo when he completed the ceiling of the Sistine Chapel?

Michelangelo was 37 years old when he completed the Sistine Chapel's ceiling.

Artistic Terms

The study and practice of art comes with its own language. Understanding some common art terms will help you to discuss your ideas about art.

abstract: based on ideas rather than reality

brushwork: the way an artist applies paint with a brush

canvas: cotton or linen cloth used as a surface for painting

ceramics: articles made from clay that has been hardened by heat

composition: the arrangement of the individual elements within a work of art so that they make a unified whole

easel: a folding stand used to hold up a painting while the artist is working

engraving: a print made from an image cut into a surface

etching: prints made from images drawn with acid-resistant material on a metal plate

form: the shape or structure of an object

gallery: a place where paintings and other works of art are exhibited and sometimes sold

medium: the materials used to create a work of art

mood: the state of mind or emotion a painting evokes

movement: a stylistic trend followed by a group of artists

permanent collection: a collection of art owned by a museum or gallery

perspective: a technique used by artists to show space

pigment: fine powder that produces color; when mixed with oil or water, it becomes paint

primary color: any of a group of colors from which all other colors can be obtained by mixing

proportion: the appropriate relation of parts to each other or to the whole artwork

space: the feeling of depth in a work of art

studio: a space, room, or building in which an artist works

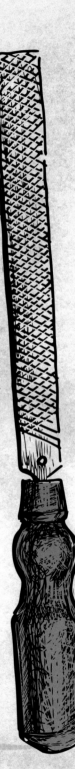

Key Words

apprentice: a person who learns a trade from a skilled employer

cadavers: dead bodies

commissions: the hiring and payment for the creation of a piece of art

foreground: the part of a picture closest to the viewer

frescoes: paintings done on wet plaster

mentors: people who provide guidance to younger or less experienced people

patron: someone who supports an artist financially

philosophy: the study of ideas about knowledge

plaster: a mixture of lime, water, and sand or cement

relief: a work of art that has parts projecting from the base

Renaissance: a cultural rebirth that took place in Europe from the 14th to 16th centuries

stencil: a device for applying a pattern or design to a surface

tempera: a permanent, fast-drying painting medium

vaulted: an arched structure

Index

Log on to www.av2books.com

AV² by Weigl brings you media enhanced books that support active learning. Go to www.av2books.com, and enter the special code found on page 2 of this book. You will gain access to enriched and enhanced content that supplements and complements this book. Content includes video, audio, weblinks, quizzes, a slide show, and activities.

AV² Online Navigation

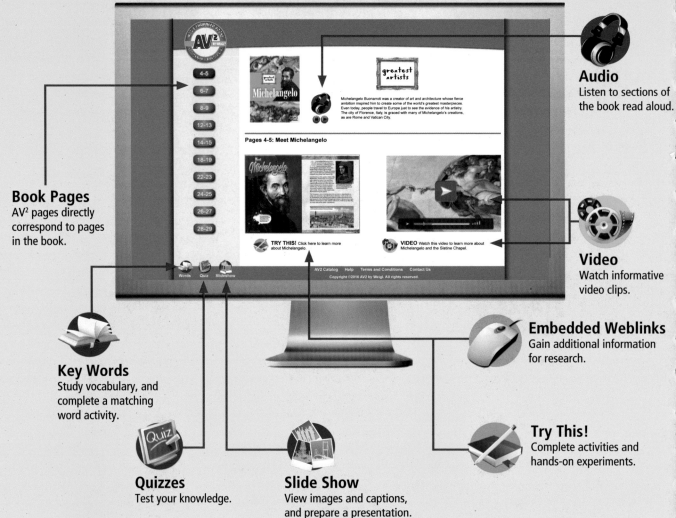

Book Pages
AV² pages directly correspond to pages in the book.

Audio
Listen to sections of the book read aloud.

Video
Watch informative video clips.

Embedded Weblinks
Gain additional information for research.

Key Words
Study vocabulary, and complete a matching word activity.

Try This!
Complete activities and hands-on experiments.

Quizzes
Test your knowledge.

Slide Show
View images and captions, and prepare a presentation.

AV² was built to bridge the gap between print and digital. We encourage you to tell us what you like and what you want to see in the future.

Sign up to be an AV² Ambassador at www.av2books.com/ambassador.